THE BEAUTIFUL STORIES

OF

THE GREAT SEAPORT (2)

...SHORT STORIES FOR RECREATIONAL READING.

....SHORT STORIES FOR COMPREHENSION LESSONS,

...ESSAYS, PROJECTS, WORKSHEETS AND ACTIVITIES.

By

DR. CHRYSTOLIVE   PRINCE

This book is the second book in a series called *The Beautiful Stories of the Great Seaport.*

The collection of all the books in this series is separately published in one book as *Short Stories of the Great Seaport by the same Arthur.*

A Publication of Redeema Inter.

Book

Two...

of the Series

God has given us two hands, one to receive with and the other to give with.

Billy Graham

Prelude

In writing one more of this series of books, I am continuing with the joyful duty of conveying one of my own distinct ways of opening my eyes to see, instead of shutting them and pretending not to see my community and the riches of our land. I would like to continue every endeavor that grants me the avenue to open my eyes wider in appreciation of others and the varied expressions of their values through their daily jobs and conscientious activities. These represent amongst other things, some noble pathways which provide due credit and grant worthy credence to people's worthwhile endeavors, their heartfelt devotions and sincere efforts to contribute to the richness of life, in whatever meaningful ways they could afford.

There is a good expression that "no one is an island". If some people were to attempt to walk through life closing their eyes, as it were, they would be denying themselves the opportunity, the privilege and grand honor of connecting well with others. By so doing, they would perhaps inadvertently, be forfeiting the full appreciation and enjoyment of all the God-given beauty and glories that surround us. High in the hierarchy of his divinely endowed riches rests the glories of his human creation in all of its terrestrial grandeur and the inestimable celestial powers.

These speak of even greater dimensions of richness and substance that calls for the depth of godly wisdom and inspiration, for the pristine revelation of that divine inner being which transients the ephemeral, outlasts the transitory and reaches for life's truest meaning, and for the salvation and fulfillment of the divine entity of immortality within of the souls of men.

Accessing and appreciating the unfathomable riches with which heaven has endowed all the beautiful lands and the blessed creatures that dwell in them, constitutes a huge portion of the very essence of living, and of enjoying and sharing the fullness of the life which the ALMIGHTY God has granted unto each one of us here, as we prepare for the inevitable hereafter.

We shall do well then to live meaningfully in our own unique way, while propelling ourselves forward towards the fullest actualization possible. Ultimately we do best by yielding centrally for the purpose of knowing our Creator with everything within our very existence, and committing ourselves totally to a lifetime of bringing him praise and glory with everything we are and in all the things we do.

If you open your eyes to see, to obverse, to ponder and also to share the best of who you are and what you are enabled by his grace to can do, you will invariably shine your light even in the darkest places and receive the joy of helping to guide someone in the right path of life. You will surely bring calmness to a bothered or grieving soul and give a warm comforting embrace to someone in need just when they need it the most. You will encourage, and yes, you will bless someone by lifting a burden even when you may not be aware of the full impact of that humble service, which you have heartily rendered in the Lord's name. You will have calmed a trembling heart and wiped off a painful tear, when only God can see the strong, devout and noble heart behind your humble service; and you will never lose your reward from the just judge of the Universe.

Therefore, remain brave as you serve your fellow human beings as you would your own brother and sisters; reach out and touch somebody in genuine love and you might happen to find you are that most needed extension of compassion and grace, the prepared instrument of God Almighty, through whom *His Holy Healing Hands* touches them, as his children for good and that forever! Blessings to you!

Chrystolive Prince

****

"He that heareth my sayings and doeth them, I will show you to whom he is like: he is like a man who built a house and dug deep and laid the foundation on a rock and when the flood rose and the stream beat vehemently upon that house, and could not shake it; for it was founded upon the rock.

But he that heareth, and doeth not, is like a man that, without a foundation built a house upon the earth, against which the stream did beat vehemently, and immediately it fell; and the ruin of that house was great".

Lk 6: 47-49

Things to Ponder

"The highest form of worship is the worship of unselfish Christian service. The greatest form of praise is the sound of consecrated feet seeking out the lost and helpless."

Billy Graham

"I do not know what I may appear to the world, but to myself I seem to have been only like a boy playing on the sea-shore, and diverting myself in now and then finding a smoother pebble or a prettier shell than ordinary, whilst the great ocean of truth lay all undiscovered before me."

– Isaac Newton

"Tact is the knack of making a point without making an enemy.

If I have seen further than others, it is by standing upon the shoulders of giants.

I can calculate the motion of heavenly bodies, but not the madness of people."

--Isaac Newton--

****

Preface

The world is spectacularly beautiful, its design is exquisite; the order and symmetry as closely constant in its organizational congruency with perfect loveliness as the closely perfect arrangement of the classic symphony in an exceptionally illuminated symmetric orchestra.

In his own words, Steve DeWitt in his outstanding book, *Eyes Wide Open: Enjoying God in Everything*, has said "Beauty was created by God for a purpose: to give us the experience of wonder. And wonder, in turn, is intended to lead us to the ultimate human expression and privilege: worship. Beauty is both a gift and a map. It is a gift to be enjoyed and a map to be followed back to the source of the beauty with praise and thanksgiving."

There are certain special geographical features in some regions of countries that distinguish them from other places. Each of those features brings to their region a distinct joy, an attraction and richness that becomes uniquely contributive to the overall blessings of the land. The United States of America is a land greatly endowed by the Lord God Almighty with many such striking and spectacular geographical landmarks. Some of these many landmarks are the Seaports of the land.

In the selective *Beautiful Stories of the Great Seaport* as well as the collective *Short Stories of the Great Seaport*, we seek to discuss the features, activities and varied contributions of a major Seaport in the

Pacific Northwest of the country. We explore the associated unique features of the Seaport, the daily activities and distinctive roles it plays in the community and regional economy, by portraying its place as one of true significance to the overall dynamic living and operational functions of the entire society.

It is notably creative of the Arthur and pleasantly enlivening to have written these *Beautiful and well-crafted Short Stories of the Great Seaport as* presented, more as a historical non-fiction, while artistically incorporating many intriguing aspects to the narrative, without tampering with the documentary flow of the overarching message. The reader will hopefully, find the stories truly enjoyable and in some places appropriately humorous without being unnecessarily satiric.

The *Beautiful Stories of The Great Seaport* and the corresponding larger collection of The Short *Stories of the Great Seaport* will hopefully challenge the young and the old alike to think more deliberatively in considering some related aspects of the inner workings of the democratic society portrayed. The considerations will equally tend to help us ponder on the subtle but challenging allusions to how we can all collaboratively help to build the society and make it work better for everyone.

The first parts of these book series have introduced us to the nature of the business of the Great Seaport and some of thrilling aspects of living near the water. We have equally deliberated on the subject of *containers* as an important equipment utilized in facilitating the job of loading and offloading the cargo at the Seaport. We shall proceed further in examining the subject of the importance of the *containers,* as well as the nature and use of the Seaport Terminals. As we do so we hope to review the need for safe storage and the importance of adequate transportation in ensuring the efficient movement of those goods from the Seaport to their final destinations.

In subsequent books in these series we shall delve even further into some other stories about the types of recreational activities people engage in within the Seaport community. These stories encourage and celebrate different kinds of recreation, competitive sports and comradery, all of which are projected as major cultural ethos by the residents of the *Great Seaport* region.

This second book in the series of the *Beautiful Stories of the Great Seaport* is one which is highly recommended as a great text for self-learners and particularly for teachers and instructors of both k-12 and higher education. It is particularly excellent for teaching (or learning) various components of Language Arts including: Reading, Creative writing, and Composition, Vocabulary and Comprehension. Many people will find them valuable instructional tools in literature, Geography , some History and titbits of Civics Each of the segmented *short stories* is followed by no less than ten comprehension questions (with those of the fifth and sixth stories merged) for easy cross-referencing and compactible workability.

These comprehension questions are well designed not only to gauge the readers' level of understanding of the text, but also to further activate critical thinking, interactive deliberations on the various issues raised in the text, as well as creative writing, comprehension answers, accurate and precise summaries and short essays.

The *Short Stories of The Great Seaport* which specifically embodies a collection of all the stories and activities of the series, also incorporates the various interactive projects briefly explored in the selective series of the short stories. The suggested projects are carved to assist the interested reader further, in learning to internalize, demonstrate and practically apply some of the key lessons of the stories. The learners and instructors will find the nature of the suggested projects to be definitely engaging, encouraging the building of cooperative learning skills, and a positive step towards the achievement of related career objectives.

 The books will also serve as excellent resources for designing, planning and successfully executing productive field trips, particularly to geographical landmarks such as a Seaport.

Therefore, read the *Beautiful Stories of the Great Seaport* and the *Short Stories of the Great Seaport* as enjoyable recreational books or read them to learn more of the functions of a *Great Seaport*. You may study each as a textbook either as a strong text for various components of Language

Arts or for some highlights in Geography, History, or titbits of related Civics.

As indicated, you may further use the books for better understanding or helpful resources for your field trips to some of the nation's seaports, their nearby cities or regions, and in particular, to the *Great Seaport* region of the Pacific Northwest. For these purposes and a lot more, read these beautiful stories.

Additionally, the book, *Beautiful Stories of the Great Seaport* or the encompassing collective *Short Stories of The Great Seaport* will help you explore further, how the commercial activities of the busy and lucrative Seaports of your country, are closely intertwined with the prosperity and economic health of not only the specific regions where they are located, but also the overall wealth and economic health of the entire land. Enjoy reading, relaxing and incorporating the applications!

Dr. Chrystolive Prince

* *

****

"When we experience a moment of beauty, we should turn wonder into worship by giving thanks to God for His goodness in providing it, for His creativity in making it, or simply for our pleasure in experiencing it...The greatest wonder is not the music itself but the Musician, not the creation but the Creator. He is beautiful."

Steve DeWitt's (*119*, 9)1.

****

'THE RELIGION OF A SAILOR '

"A sea captain when he stands upon the bridge, or looks out from his deck-house, thinks much about God and about the world. Away in the valley yonder among the corn and the poppies men may well forget all things except the warmth of the sun upon the face, and the kind shadow under the hedge; but he who journeys through storm and darkness must needs think and think... One July a couple of years ago I took my supper with a Captain Moran on board the s.s. *Margaret*, that had put into a western river from I know not where. I found him a man of many notions all flavored with his personality, as is the way with sailors. He talked in his queer sea manner **of God and the world**, and up through all his words broke the hard energy of his calling."

William Butler Yeats, *The Celtic Twilight--*

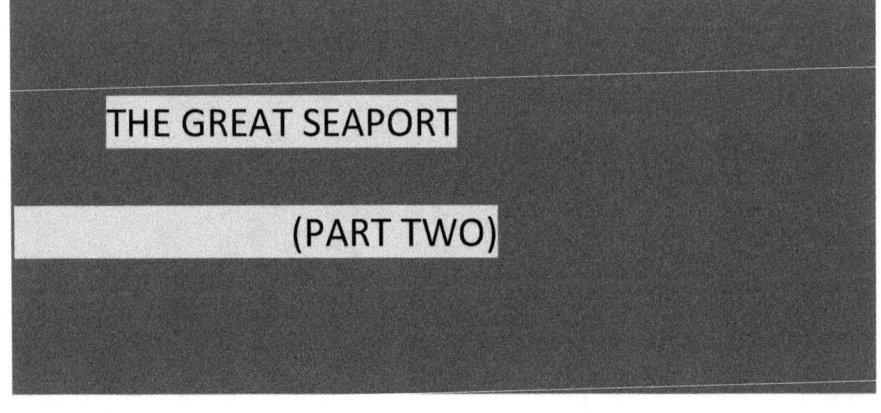

THE GREAT SEAPORT

(PART TWO)

Hello, this is your good friend Benjamin Polito once again, ready to share with you more of the *Beautiful Stories of the Great Seaport.* Today I am relaxing as usual, outside my home and watching *the Great Seaport,* with people streaming in and out, which makes it look much like an anthill. I am looking at a 600ft ship that has just anchored at the harbor, which would surely guarantee very busy container terminals for days on end. Container terminals are the places where ships dock to load and unload their cargo.

This particular ship, like numerous others which anchor at the harbors of this Seaport is a big one. Consequently, the Seaport employees will be busy and sure to have moved literarily thousands of containers by the time the cargo has been fully taken off the ship and transported away to their various destinations. The available areas for the Port operations is comprised of well over one thousand and some hundreds of acres of waterfront land and nearby properties, which would include container terminals, general cargo terminals, foreign trade zone, break-bulk and refrigerated cargo and storage.

The Seaport is well managed although its operations are quite complex, which also includes ensuring the successful management of hundreds of cruise ships, serving no less than seven different cruise lines and over one million cruise passengers that pass through its facilities every year.

Each cruise line brings enormous commercial activity and significant returns on the financial investment into this segment of the Seaport operations. It is estimated that each cruise line brings several millions of dollars to the local economy, which results in the overall cruise industry generating several hundreds of millions of dollars in annual business revenue. This is in conjunction with the creation of thousands of good paying jobs for the residents of the surrounding region.

Furthermore, the effeciently run cruise terminals, coupled with many provisions for convenient cruise and air travel connections provide many opportunities for trans-regional, inter-state and international business connections. There remains also the enjoyment of touring the beautiful compact surrounding city with her thriving shopping facilities, lively cuisines, fine Northwest wines and of course, the city's widely famous coffee.

There are in addition, attractive scenic gardens and glass, fresh fish and natural produce market, historic square and space needle attractions conveniently close to the waterfront of the famous Seaport. Undoubtedly, these added provisions have esterblished the Great Seaport as a preferred choice for many who love to travel through the city to other destinations in the Northwest and beyond to some other related regions of the world.

****

****

****

Carnival Miracle at Smith Cove Cruise Terminal

"The planning stage of a cruise is often just as enjoyable as the voyage itself, letting one's imagination loose on all kinds of possibilities. Yet translating dreams into reality means a lot of practical questions have to be answered."

- Jimmy Cornell (World Cruising Handbook--

OCEAN CARRIER

Container Seaport

In this remarkable city, *the Great Seaport's* 27 container cranes move over two million containers a year which makes the Port one of the busiest container Seaports not only in the United States but also inarguably within the whole wide world. Along with all of its accomplishments, *the Great Seaport* remains environmentally friendly, currently claiming the enviable reputation of offering the lowest carbon footprint for cargo shipped by sea from some foreign regions such as Asia, to major markets in the Eastern and Midwestern parts of the United States.

It is an important educational, enlightening and enjoyable experience to actually watch the ships dock and observe first-hand the container operations. In the event that you are unable like I do, to watch from the vicinity of your own private property, you will be welcome to find out the ship schedules from the Port Authority staff and plan your visit ahead of time, to be when the ship of your interest is due in the Port.

Several Port parks offer excellent viewpoints from where you can clearly see container operations. The hours of operations of the parks are sufficiently flexible to suit most of your convenience, even when you include overriding factors such as unforeseen emergencies or probable restrictions imposed by weather variations.

****

**************************************(

(((

(((

Central Terminal at the nearby Airport

Grain and Breakbulk Terminals

It is also important to note as I have observed, that there are some goods that are offloaded from the ships with other kinds of equipment other than containers. Some softer, more perishable goods such as apples (this particular region of the American Pacific Northwest is renowned for producing some of the best apples and pears in the entire nation) and grains are able to be shipped in bulk forms without containers.

The Great Seaport has some special terminals (such as the grain terminals) to handle these kinds of goods. Today, I have observed that grains were being loaded with chutes directly into the ships from the grain terminals. The fully-automated grain facility proudly provides a wide range of electronic controls and mechanical devices that assure the efficient movement of grain from railcars and trucks through silos to ships' hold. This terminal is extensive with a capacity for four million bushels elevator and can accommodate trucks and railcars in addition to sea-going vessels.

The terminal's vast acres of fully paved fence storage which runs the full length of the wharf are equally fully equipped with two electric-belt conveyor systems, along with five loading spouts and two direct-transfer drag conveyor systems for direct rail-to-sip transfers. The modernized Terminals' operations of the Great Seaport enables this facility to be fully functional, currently holding close to seventy silos with the capacity for over a dozen thousand bushels each, and several dozens of interstices with the large capacity of approximately fourteen thousand bushels each.

The grain terminal systems much like other terminal facilities in the Great Seaport are specially constructed to yield for further industrial and technological extensions. Consequently, they would be

progressively highly modernized, being
built to be expandable beyond the current
four-million-bushel capacity.

We must note that through these separately
designed and efficiently operated terminals, the
Port as a whole has expanded its capabilities to
strengthen in a more comprehensive manner,
the United States trade flows. This remarkable
achievement is in addition to setting new
standards for grain exports across the entire
nation and beyond the country to regions
abroad.

Similarly, the *Great Seaport* has multiple well-
constructed, equipped and functional
warehouses for the storage of various other

products. Examples of the other products are wood and paper. The breakbulk terminal facilities which are fully equipped to support large operations and special projects are utilized to ship and receive both international and domestic import and export cargo. The Seaport proudly reports that one of its multiple large breakbulk cargo terminals holds about twelve hundred feet "of in three berths at the main pier (with alongside depth of 9 meters (30 feet) and 121 meters (400 feet) of berthing space in one berth at the finger pier with alongside depth of 15 meters (50 feet)... equipped with top-lift trucks, heavy and smaller forklifts, and crawler cranes".

This notable record is in addition to a separate breakbulk cargo facility that offers short- and long-term moorage breakbulk reefer vessels, roll-on and roll-off vessels, commercial workboats, fishing vessels, tugs, barges, ferries, and factory trawlers.

The Great Seaport would boast that this particular multiple dozens hectare cargo terminal which is fully equipped with heavy-lift float cranes, forklifts, and other equipment "has about eight thousand feet of (8000 feet) of moorage with new concrete aprons, large staging areas, and on-dock rail service". The terminal is also built to offers bunker fuel, fish processing and cold storage services with rail access to the adjacent BNSF mainline and classification yard. Fortunately, the facility equally has direct access to both the Union Pacific and two major Interstate Highways {highway 5 and 90} for efficient facilitation of interstate commerce.

The Great Seaport area is a natural location for

trans-loading as well as regional distribution of cargo to other major regional markets.

OPERATIONAL PARTNERSHIP

The Northwest Seaport Alliance is a marine cargo joint operating partnership of the two major divisions of the Great Seaport which form one of the few largest container gateways in the North American continent. Whereas the Great Seaport area is a natural location for trans-loading as well as regional distribution of cargo to other major regional markets, this operational alliance ensures the maintenance of excellent services in the enumerated divisions.

The regional commercial and economic needs are thus well protected as much the understandable national interests, especially as the Great Seaport is the closest of major United States Ports to Asia and the key gateway to the expansive state of Alaska. In addition the Port regularly offers crucial services to Hawaii and Guam.

The famous Northwest Seaport Alliance also provides numerous direct international trade links through regular container carrier services to Europe, Asia

Central & South America, and Oceania. The Alliance regularly grants scheduled liner services connecting cargo to dozens of direct international Ports of call, including breakbulk and Ro/Ro carriers. This is in addition to numerous similar services to united domestic markets in the Pacific Northwest region of the United States and beyond.

Along these lines, the Great Seaport being one of the largest container Ports in North America, have attracted the investment of huge sums of money both for the construction and updating of the terminals and the upgrading of road infrastructure, especially the major interstate highways and intermodal rails, which must handle expanding volumes of cargo storage and distribution. This extensive modernization {which includes the upgrade of power, dock and berth for all terminals} is indisputably crucial for servicing bigger ships and larger vessels, along with the corresponding utilization of more efficient super-post-Panamax cranes.

Super-post Panamax and Automobiles

It is important to underscore the fact, the super-post Panamax and other similar capacity cranes hold more advanced capabilities that can service 10,000-TEU and larger vessels. The employment of full capacity cranes of this nature are quite beneficial, as they help sustain huge Seaport operations and support the maintenance of a collaborative, business friendly relationship with the merchants and vast pool of customers which the Great Seaport must serve.

There are also as you might expect, huge expansive parking areas, within the vicinity of the *Great Seaport* for imported machinery and automobiles. There are many people who like me like good trucks and there are plenty of excellent models and designs one could choose from at any given time. Sometimes, like today, when I watch the most modern, brand new beautiful automobiles being offloaded, I suddenly wish that I could simply forget about my older rugged automobile and go immediately and get one of the very attractive new ones.

Fortunately, I have learned the hard way to keep my emotions under control. This is because, I have come to understand the importance of remaining disciplined and exercising self-control in many aspects of life. As a result, I personally realize that I cannot always jump up and get or buy whatever I want, just whenever and wherever I feel like doing so.

Moreover, if you live near a Great Seaport, like I do, where a wide variety of product inventory and inviting goods are constantly processed, you might get close enough to losing your mind if you keep holding on to the tendency to shop uncontrollably. This will be especially the case if your financial position requires that you must have to keep an eye on the limitations of funds in your bank accounts! It is important to always endeavor to live within your budget and to remember the old adage—*'good things never finish'.*

I have decided that if I work hard, continue to fear and honor God and live a decent life, I can save up money to buy what is necessary, such as a car of my choice when I really need it and can afford it. Consequently, it will always be an automobile that fits into my budget. A good, strong, nice durable car is very important, and that is what I usually go for more than super-fanciful exteriors_ although I am not entirely discounting the importance of nice exteriors.

More importantly, I am emphasizing that a well-meaning individual cannot always simply go around trying to buy the whole world at impulse. We should concede the fact there are also other important things to take care of besides driving around in nice expensive cars.

Moreover, it is equally good to remember other people who are in need and to endeavor to give a helping hand to other people in less fortunate circumstances than ourselves. We could all keep in mind and never forget, that much more often than not, many people in difficult circumstances and less than desirable life situations, do suffer terribly and unjustifiably due to certain circumstances beyond their control. It is noteworthy that sometimes as a society, we spend a lot of time in discussing the plight of such individuals and even more time in proposing how best to deal with the difficulties which they suffer; but at the end, after all said and done, there is often more said than done!

As a society, we should not underestimate the difference that the contribution of well-meaning individuals can make in the lives of the people in need. I have said all these amongst other reasons, to underscore the importance of well-meaning individuals like you and myself making *compassionate and conscientious efforts to assist our fellow citizens and neighbors.* At the same time, my encouragement does not necessarily seek to discount the importance of the role of big corporations in responding to the needs of people going through difficult times or the meaningful contributions of the society as a whole through the government.

Instead, I am further encouraging the continued participation of everyone in the best ways we could, in the act of giving, showing mercy and helping to bear one another's burdens. There is a depth of inward satisfaction and unique richness of faith in reaching out to touch others with kindness, especially when those people are struggling and suffering and would benefit much from the understanding and encouragement of many others around them. The Words of the **Great Book, The**

Holy Bible, as written is true and readily come to mind:

"But to do well and to share, forget not; for with such sacrifices God is well-pleased." 2

"Godliness with contentment is great gain." 3

And

"Ye ought to support the weak, and to remember the words of the Lord Jesus, how he said, It is more blessed to give than to receive." Acts 20:35. 4

Norwegian Pearl at terminal

****

COMPREHENSION QUESTIONS

****

1. State three distinct features of the Great Seaport that make it an important economic contributor to the regional economy.

How does each of these factors enable the Port to play a major role in the national economy?

2. What constitutes the main difference between the way other terminals receive their goods and the process of transferring products to the grain terminals? Why do you consider it important for the Port to differentiate the types of equipment utilized in loading and offloading softer cargo like grains?

3. Are there additional risks associated with the processing of consumable products like gains and apples? Explain your answer with illustrations.

4. Have you ever boarded a cruise ship or cruised by sea? If yes, share your

experiences using illustrations or *presentation.*

5. Alternatively would you like to take a trip to the Great Seaport or any other major Seaport? Explore and outline the advantages of travelling or vacationing by cruise ships.

6. What do you find to be six main reasons why many people love to travel through the Great Seaport and the nieghboring city, to their destinations in the Northwest and some other related regions of the world?

7. Outline the major factors that would have led to the decision to build the

various separate terminals in the *Great Seaport?*

8. In what specific ways does the *Great Seaport* contribute to the overall standard of living within the United States and conversely that the rest of the world? Why do you think this particular Seaport is regarded as the commercial hub or center of this region?

9. What are the advantages and possible disadvantages of living near a major Seaport?

10. Discuss the probable meaning of the adage –'*good things do not finish*'.

11. What do you think could be the practical applications of this statement to you personally?

12. What would be the possible implications to you and your friends of ignoring the principle implied in this statement?

9. Discuss the meaning of the quotes in the above story taken from the *BIG BOOK*. What *BIG BOOK* is the Arthur referring to?

And why do you think it is often referred to as, **THE BIG BOOK**?

10. Discuss the probable applications of the referenced quote (for you and others)— *'godliness with contentment is great gain'.*

11. Further discuss the practical application of the other quote in the story—

'It is more blessed to give than to receive'.

12. What do you consider to be the most important ways you could give or become a blessing to another person?

***What is the most valuable or indispensable gift of all?

))

88888888888888888888888888888888

****8888888****88888888888*****888

Looking Forward

****

Admittedly, we have had some good communication about the purpose of containers and their importance in the functions and contribution of the Great Seaport to the regional commerce. In addition, we need to spend time discussing further, especially on **the succeeding books of this series**, how those goods delivered *through* the containers actually *get from the Great Seaport to their final destinations in order to benefit the general consumers in the society.*

The journey of the containers which we shall discuss in other books of this series is quite facscinatiing. We intend to methodologically chronicle the way the various goods are transported, after they are received at the beautiful Great Seaport, all the way to their final destinations where such goods are eventually delivered for various uses by the citizenry.

Sometimes the goods are temporarily stored in the Great Seaport facilities before they are sent on thier journey. Notably, the journey itself represents a crucial operational component which must ensure that through divers forms of safe transportation and routes, the delivery of goods are made on schedule and often as quickly as possible, for the needs of the people in the communities and for the general welfare of the broader society.

On other occasions, the goods may be uploaded soon after they are offloaded from *the ships, directly unto trucks and other means of transportation and speedily sent to thier designated destinations, where the consumers would be eagerly waiting to recieve their machandise.*

****

****

****

Food for your Thoughts

****

Projects and assignments that are constructive, manual, artistic and creative will have an added advantage in the process of intellectually encoding and permanently internalizing the learned concepts. It is helpful to present the instruction in a coherent, concise and sequential manner, thereby ensuring that the subject matter learned is properly integrated into the overall body of information. This will assist not only when educators must necessarily engage in curricular assessment and evaluation, but more importantly, in the timely recollection and practical application of the important knowledge gained.

The vast content of knowledge gained in this manner ultimately will never be wasted, even when it is not apparently assessed or overtly applied in the short run. Recollection and productive utilization of the internalized knowledge will often become necessary and quite helpful in more ways than one; the applicability being incorporated and processed through the mainstream of a myriad of complex body of information, will typically serve in multiple salient ways in developing and equipping the learned individual for productive living and service to the society.

It is hoped that both the segmented stories presented as Beautiful Stories of the Great Seaport, *and the collective larger book,* Short Stories of the Great Seaport *will offer enriching blessings and contribute significantly to such collective body of knowledge.*

Rich Blessings to every reader!

Dr. Chrystolive

References

1. THE HOLY BIBLE (KJV) *All scriptural references

2. Steve DeWitt's outstanding book, *Eyes Wide Open: Enjoying God in Everything*, Credo House, 2012. 91

3. ***Hebrews 13:16***

4. ***I Timothy 6:6***

5. ***Acts 20:35***

ACKNOWLEGEMENT

I acknowledge with appreciation both the photographer Don Wilson, other officials of the *Port of Seattle* in general, for the helpful contribution, through the courtesy of the excellent photographs and the provision of other relevant information towards the successful publication of the *Beautiful Stories of the Great Seaport* as well as *Short Stories of the Great Seaport.*

This publication is a series

To be continued in *The Beautiful Stories of the*

*Great Sea*port: Book Three

**Short Stories of The Great Seaport:
*short stories for recreation, comprehension
lessons, worksheets, projects & activities,* by the
same Author **CHRYSTOLIVE PRINCE**

Amazon.com and on *Createspace.com.*
Kindle

HE ALMIGHTY WILL DEFEND US

www.ingramcontent.com/pod-product-compliance
Lightning Source LLC
Chambersburg PA
CBHW070109210526
45170CB00013B/801